Finding 3-D Shapes in
New York City

Julia Wall

Real World Math Books are published by Capstone Press,
151 Good Counsel Drive, P.O. Box 669, Mankato, Minnesota 56002.
www.capstonepress.com

062011
006228WZVMI

Books published by Capstone Press are manufactured with paper
containing at least 10 percent post-consumer waste.

Library of Congress Cataloging-in-Publication Data
Wall, Julia.
  Finding 3-D shapes in New York City / by Julia Wall.
    p. cm. -- (Real world math)
  Includes index.
  ISBN 978-1-4296-5189-9 (lib. bdg.)
  1. Geometry in architecture--Juvenile literature. 2. Shapes--Juvenile literature. 3. Problem solving--
    Juvenile literature. I. Title. II. Title: Finding three-D shapes in New York City.
  NA2760.W35 2009
  701'.8--dc22

                                                                              2009051381

0128

Editorial Credits
Sara Johnson, editor; Emily R. Smith, M.A.Ed., editorial director; Sharon Coan, M.S.Ed., editor-in-chief;
Lee Aucoin, creative director; Rachelle Cracchiolo, M.S.Ed., publisher

Photo Credits
The author and publisher would like to gratefully credit or acknowledge the following for permission
to reproduce copyright material: cover, Big Stock Photos; title, Photodisc; p.4 (below), Photodisc; p.4
(above), Shutterstock; p.6, Photodisc; p.7, Corbis; p.8, Big Stock Photos; p.9, Elvele Images/Alamy;
p.10, Corbis; p.11, Kevin Foy/Alamy; p.12, Jochen Tack/Alamy; p.13, Corbis; p.14, Visions of America,
LLC/Alamy; p.15, Visions of America, LLC/Alamy; p.16, I Stock Photos; p.17, NYCFoto.com; p.18,
Shutterstock; p.19, NYCFoto.com; p.20, Corbis; p.21, Stock Connection Blue/Alamy; p.22, Getty Images;
p.23, Alex Segre/Alamy; p.24 (left), Photodisc; p.24 (right), Ken Welsh/Alamy; p.25, Alice McBroom;
p.26 (above), Photodisc; p.26 (below left), Shutterstock; p.26 (below right), Big Stock Photos; p.27
(above), Big Stock Photos; p.27 (below right), Shutterstock; p.27 (below left), Corbis RF; p.29, Big
Stock Photos

While every care has been taken to trace and acknowledge copyright, the publishers tender their
apologies for any accidental infringement where copyright has proved untraceable. They would be
pleased to come to a suitable arrangement with the rightful owner in each case.

Table of Contents

A Vacation in New York City

I am spending my vacation in New York City with my uncle. He is going to take me on a tour of the city.

Hunting for 3-D Shapes

I'm learning about 3-D shapes right now in school. My uncle says we will find lots of 3-D shapes in New York. I can't wait!

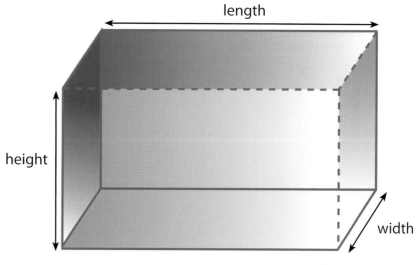

rectangular prism

What Are 3-D Shapes?
3-D means three-dimensional. The **dimensions** (duh-MEN-shuhns) of a 3-D shape are length, width, and height.

Scraping the Sky

New York is full of **skyscrapers**. Many skyscrapers are rectangular **prisms**. Rectangular prisms are 3-D shapes made up of rectangles.

LET'S EXPLORE MATH

3-D shapes have faces. The faces are the flat parts of a 3-D shape.

Look at the rectangular prism above. How many faces does it have?

This is the Seagram Building. It is a huge rectangular prism. It has 6 rectangular faces.

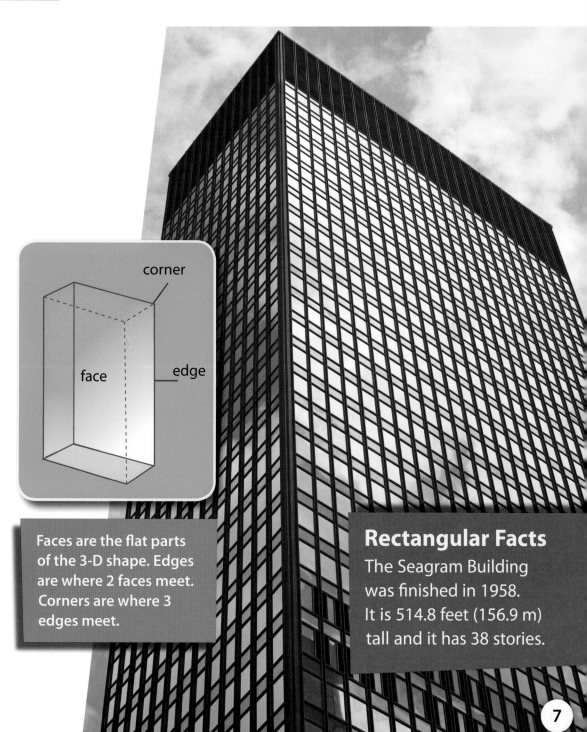

corner

face   edge

Faces are the flat parts of the 3-D shape. Edges are where 2 faces meet. Corners are where 3 edges meet.

Rectangular Facts
The Seagram Building was finished in 1958. It is 514.8 feet (156.9 m) tall and it has 38 stories.

An Unusual Building

My favorite skyscraper is the Flatiron Building. It is different from most other skyscrapers. It is an unusual shape for a skyscraper.

Shape Up

Some **architects** like to use certain shapes in their buildings. Some like to design buildings with **curved** shapes. Others like flat, straight shapes.

The Flatiron Building is a triangular prism. It has 5 faces. Its edges are curved a little.

Triangular Facts

The real name of the Flatiron Building is the Fuller Building. It is 285 feet (87 m) tall.

LET'S EXPLORE MATH

Look at the photo above.

a. How many faces of the Flatiron building can you see in this photo?

b. How many faces are hidden?

A Glass Cube

Next, I wanted to find a cube. It was hard! But we found this amazing store.

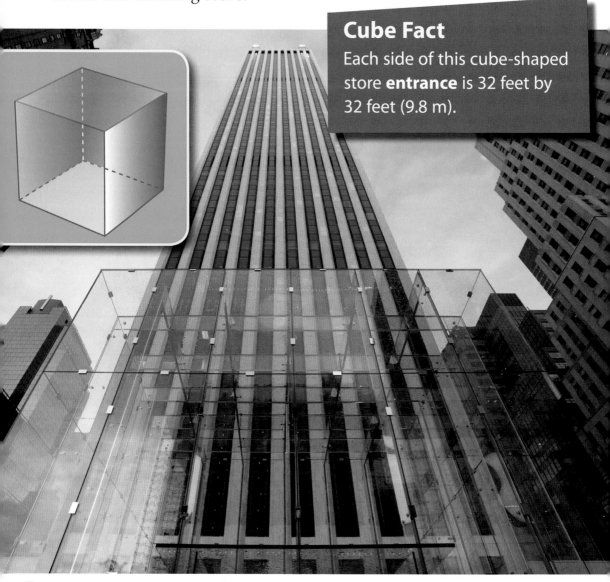

Cube Fact

Each side of this cube-shaped store **entrance** is 32 feet by 32 feet (9.8 m).

This store also has an elevator in the shape of a **cylinder**.

The store is underground and the entrance is a big glass cube. It has 6 faces, all the same size.

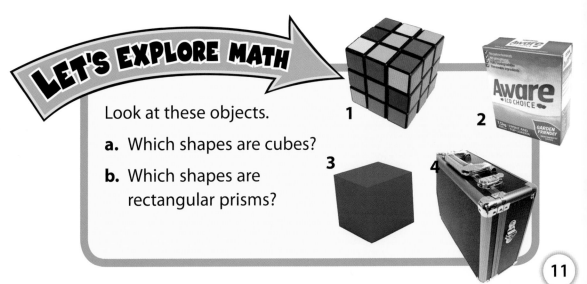

LET'S EXPLORE MATH

Look at these objects.

a. Which shapes are cubes?

b. Which shapes are rectangular prisms?

1

2

3

4

Columns Are Cylinders

I wondered where we would find a cylinder. My uncle said he would take me to Columbus Circle. It has a statue of Christopher Columbus.

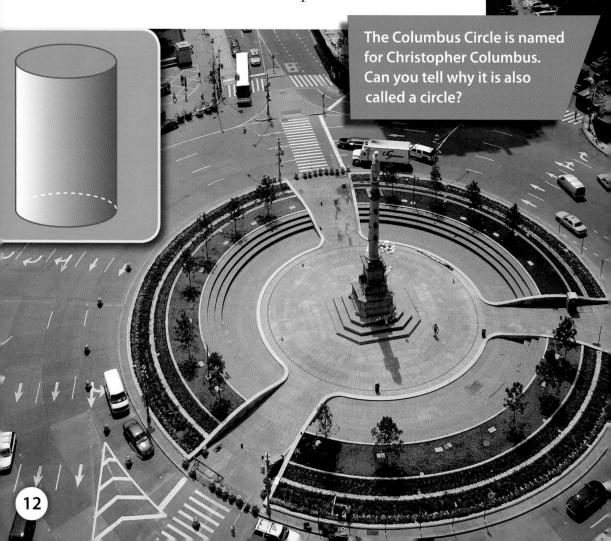

The Columbus Circle is named for Christopher Columbus. Can you tell why it is also called a circle?

The statue sits on top of a column. A column is a cylinder. It has 2 circular faces and a curved side.

Cylinder Fact
The cylinder that holds up the Columbus statue is 70 feet (21.3 m) high.

A Round Sculpture

Right near the cylinder, we found a **sphere**. This sphere is a **sculpture** of Earth. It is made of metal.

This sculpture of Earth sits outside Trump Tower.

The Earth sculpture has only 1 curved side. It does not have edges or corners. A sphere doesn't have a face, so there is a pole to stop it from rolling away!

LET'S EXPLORE MATH

Look at these sphere and cylinder shapes.

a. What is the same about these 2 shapes?

b. What is different?

A Cone Forest

Next we went to Central Park. We walked through a part of the park that was like a forest. There were over 400 pine trees. I found a lot of cones—pine cones!

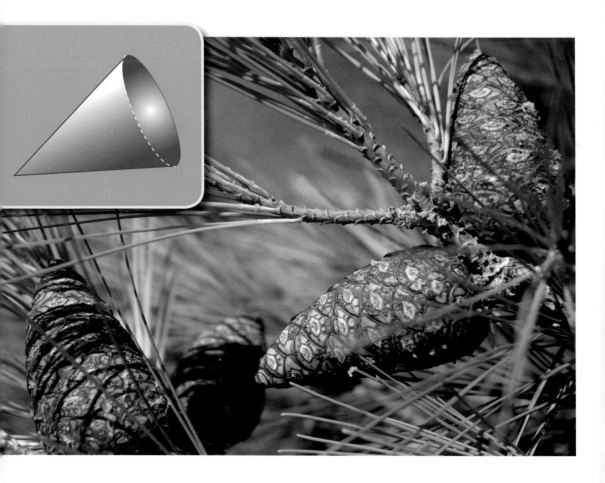

Pine cones are cone-shaped. A cone has 1 circular face and a curved side. The point of a cone is called the **vertex**.

This part of Central Park is called the Ross Pinetum. It was named after Arthur Ross, who gave money for the trees to be planted.

Egypt or New York?

I bet you thought there were no pyramids in New York. Well, take a look at the top of this building!

This building is called One Worldwide Plaza.

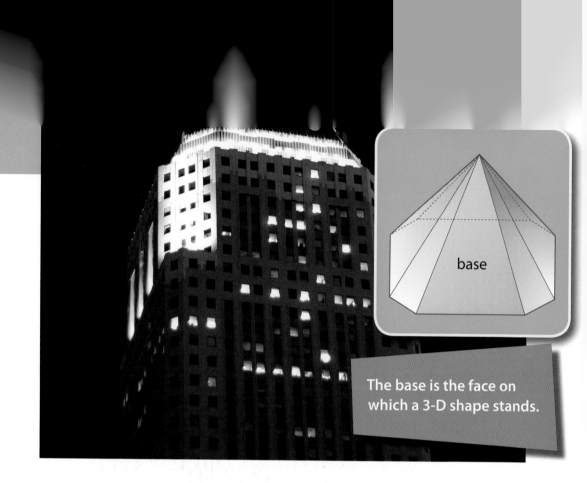

base

The base is the face on which a 3-D shape stands.

One Worldwide Plaza has a pyramid on top. This special pyramid has 9 faces. There are 8 side faces and 1 base.

LET'S EXPLORE MATH

Look at this pyramid.

a. How many triangles can you see?

b. What other shape can you see that is not a triangle?

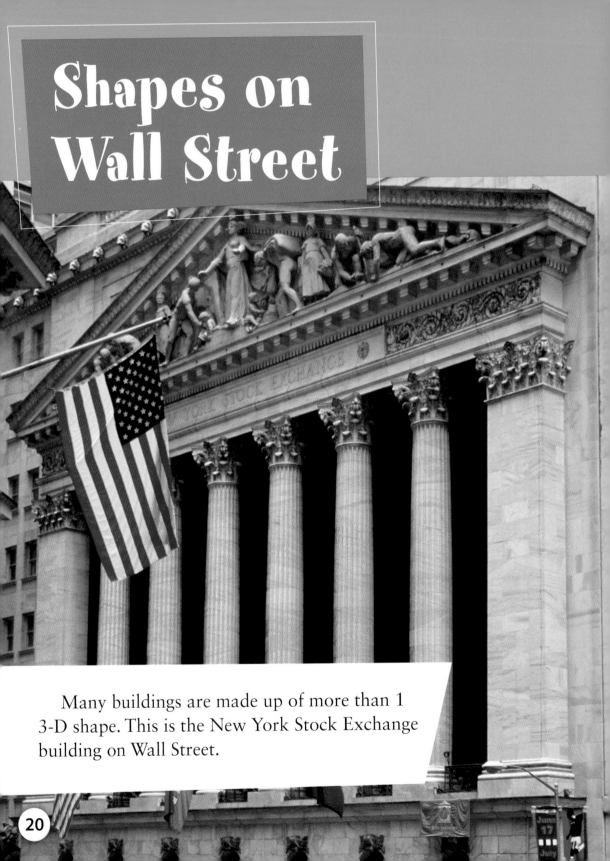

Shapes on Wall Street

Many buildings are made up of more than 1 3-D shape. This is the New York Stock Exchange building on Wall Street.

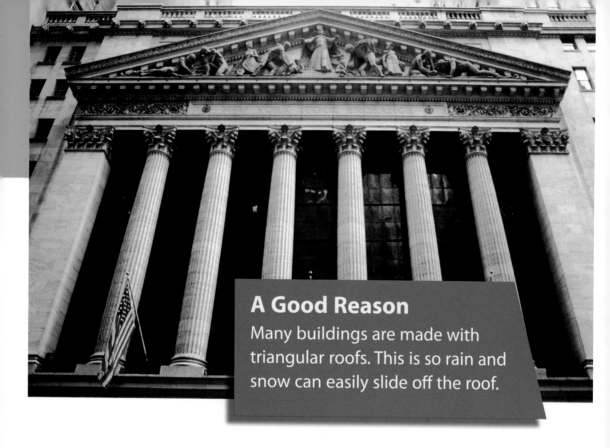

This building has a triangular prism above the columns. The prism is held up by 6 cylinders. Each cylinder has 2 circular faces and 1 curved side.

LET'S EXPLORE MATH

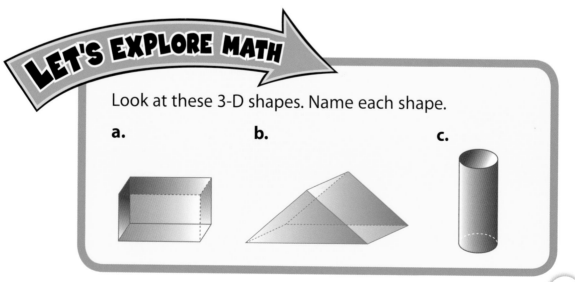

Look at these 3-D shapes. Name each shape.

a.

b.

c.

Many Shapes

The New York Mosque is another building with many 3-D shapes. It has cubes and rectangular prisms. It also has a circular **dome** as part of the roof.

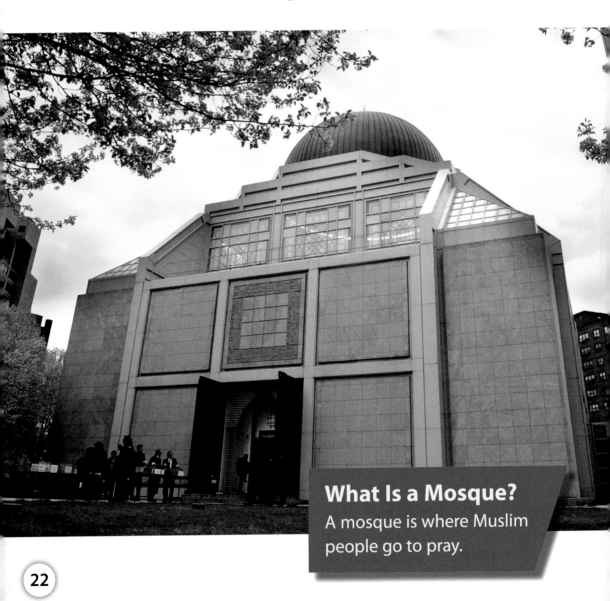

What Is a Mosque?
A mosque is where Muslim people go to pray.

This is the San Remo apartment building. Can you see the cylinders on this building?

The San Remo has 2 towers in the shape of rectangular prisms. Each tower is 10 stories high.

23

I also saw many smaller 3-D shapes all over New York. My uncle bought me a soda. And I realized soda comes in a cylinder!

Then I had some ice cream. My ice cream was sitting on a cone!

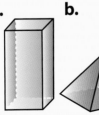

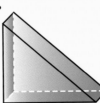

LET'S EXPLORE MATH

Name the 2-D shapes that are found on the faces of these 3-D shapes.

a.　　　b.　　　c.　　　　　　d.　　　e.

Even my guidebook was a rectangular prism.

There are 3-D shapes all over New York City. They can be seen on buildings, in parks, and on the street.

So how many 3-D shapes can you find in your town? What about in your home? I bet your home is full of 3-D shapes.

Making Shapes

Jackson wants to draw an octagonal prism. To do this he needs to know how many faces, edges, and corners there are. Can you work it out?

Solve It!

Step 1: Look at the prisms. Then draw this table and fill in how many faces, edges, and corners each 3-D shape has. Some of them have been done for you.

Prism	Faces	Edges	Corners
triangular	5	9	6
rectangular	6	12	8
pentagonal		15	
hexagonal	8		12
heptagonal		21	14
octagonal			

?

Step 2: Look for a pattern for the number of faces. Continue the pattern to find the number of faces in an octagonal prism.

Step 3: Look for a pattern for the number of edges. Continue the pattern to find the number of edges in an octagonal prism.

Step 4: Look for a pattern for the number of corners. Continue the pattern to find the number of corners in an octagonal prism.

Step 5: Draw an octagonal prism.

Glossary

architects—people who design, or draw, buildings

curved—rounded, like a ball

cylinder—a 3-D shape with 2 round faces and 1 curved side

dimensions—measurements of shapes; 3-D shapes have height, length, and width.

dome—a shape used in building that looks like a half of a sphere

entrance—an opening or doorway

prisms—3-D shapes with straight sides

sculpture—an artwork made by modeling, carving, or constructing shapes from clay, stone, wood, or metal

skyscrapers—very tall buildings; they look as if they "scrape" the sky

sphere—a 3-D shape with a curved side and no face

vertex—a point where 2 or more lines meet

Index

Internet Sites

FactHound offers a safe, fun way to find Internet sites related to this book. All of the sites on FactHound have been researched by our staff.

Here's all you do:

Visit *www.facthound.com*

FactHound will fetch the best sites for you!

31

Let's Explore Math

Page 6:
The rectangular prism has 6 faces.

Page 9:
a. You can see 3 faces. **b.** There are 2 hidden faces.

Page 11:
a. Shapes 1 and 3 are cubes.
b. Shapes 1, 2, 3 and 4 are rectangular prisms.

Page 15:
a. Both shapes have a curved side.
b. Answers may vary but could include "a cylinder has 2 faces but a sphere has no face."

Page 19:
a. 4 triangles **b.** A square

Page 21:
a. A rectangular prism
b. A triangular prism
c. A cylinder

Page 24:
a. Rectangles (and squares) **b.** Triangles and rectangles
c. Rectangles and triangles **d.** Circle **e.** Circles (and rectangle)

Problem-Solving Activity:

Prism	Faces	Edges	Corners
triangular	5	9	6
rectangular	6	12	8
pentagonal	7	15	10
hexagonal	8	18	12
heptagonal	9	21	14
octagonal	10	24	16

An octagonal prism has 10 faces, 24 edges, and 16 corners.